AF499554

Arthur de Niet holds a Master degree (MSc) in the field of Business Engineering & Management Information Systems and has been working throughout his career in the Oil and Gas industry in both Europe and Latin America.

While working in different parts of the world he noticed the importance of solid financial education and therefore started to write books and eBooks to explain the importance of common sense in doing business and the often forgotten simple financial basics which he applies into different models.

Since 2012 he has been working in the field of corporate IT Portfolio Management and has gained a lot of insightful experiences which he shares in this book.

Arthur currently lives in The Netherlands, is married and is the father of three children.

"It is sometimes shocking to see how people accept the reduction of control on their (financial) future by only focusing on the reality of today" – **Arthur de Niet**

Integral IT Portfolio Management

Insight in Value & Costs of IT Systems

Arthur de Niet

AlanoPress, Netherlands

This edition is published in 2015 by AlanoPress

Published 2015 by Arthur de Niet, The Netherlands
For information contact: contact@itpfm.com
www.alanopress.com

ISBN/EAN: 978-90-824839-0-1

Printed and Distributed by Lulu.com

To all the people that I have met throughout my education and career that helped me shaping my life the way it is. I would like to name a few people specifically for their significant contribution: first of all my family, who are always there and keep me focused on what is really important in life. In addition Paul, Rupen and Marcelo for working with me on the topic IT Portfolio Management and the creation of this book.

Preface

Thank you for buying this book or perhaps you got it as a present. This book is an introduction of how to get more insight and control on your IT landscape and initiate the thought process of what that IT landscape is actually worth to your organization. Or in other words; **what is the value of IT?** What is the added value that the IT landscape or IT system brings to your organization? And **what does IT cost**? And is that in balance? In order to answer these questions it's needed to gain full insight and control over all IT components there are the IT landscape in question and the related costs and expenses. In many ways it will be a similar journey when you want to get grip on your personal financial situation at home. It all, at the end, comes down to the (boring) details of all your expenses.

If you are already fully in control of your IT finances, than hereby my sincere congratulations; you have already achieved what this book is aiming for. In that case; please pass on this book to someone you know, who's organization is not in full control yet. In any case; this book is an introduction to the Methodology ITPfM (Integrated IT Portfolio Management) which is an integral approach to gain insight into all your IT components and their related expenses. The aim is to help you as a reader understand how much value IT brings to your organization and how much it actually costs. This will enable you, for example, to better able to make IT decisions (replacement & investments) and in addition able to cut costs where needed/desired. With already so many IT management books in the market; why a book about IT Portfolio Management? This is a question I have been ask many times. My answer to this question is; organizations need to go back to the basics on IT spending, like sometimes you need to do in your private household, to spend time and analyze what you are paying for and why? With the fast way we are now able to collect and interpret information it is now possible to start creating an integral view on IT within a company based on concrete and real-time data. Software vendors like SAP, IBM, HP (but there are many others in the market) are aiming at the integration of all IT supported business functions into one Enterprise solution. Major/Global companies are therefore now better able to have a real-time integral view on how the company is performing, no matter where its factories are located. However, one important element in the above development was kept outside this integral view; which was the IT function and solutions itself. IT was (and often still is) not seen as a core pillar of the business and therefore is not managed the same way the core business functions like sales, production, finance and logistics are managed. This results in the situation that in many companies each function or business unit has its own IT department that has the freedom to use software dedicated to that specific business process or function for efficiency and reductions in costs to stay competitive. All this works very well, at least as long as the company is able to afford IT this way. However, with the current economic changes companies are forced to look deeper into their spending, just like you would do in your private situation. Therefore, it's only a natural next step that companies are now also more looking at IT to understand the added value IT brings and how much it costs.

The integral ITPfM methodology is developed to gain clarity and insight about how IT is organized in an organization and how it adds value to the company, combined with how expensive the IT solutions are both from an operational perspective and an investment/project perspective. It combines all elements related to IT management (Investment, Operations, Projects and Technology development) into a single integrated model, which provides an Integral view of the IT landscape and the total costs of owning IT. This book is written for everyone that works in IT organizations and looking for opportunities to reduce of costs and waste in IT landscapes and to understand better the value IT brings to the organization.

Content

Preface

Part 1: Introduction to ITPfM

ITPfM – IT Portfolio Management

ITPfM – Quick Self-Assessment

Part 2 ITPfM Methodology

Chapter 1 Integrated ITPfM Value/Cost Model

- ITPfM Integrated Value/Cost Model
- Business Process or Function
- ITPfM IT Value Model
- ITPfM Quadrant & IT portfolio
- ITPfM Quadrant & Blocks
- How the different ITPfM Quadrant Blocks work together

Part 3 Roll out of IT Portfolio Management

Chapter 2 Is your organization ready?

Chapter 3 ITPfM Organization – creation of a single IT organization

- Creation of a single IT function
- ITPfM Roles within IT Portfolio

Chapter 4 Introduction of a single truth - Work with trusted Information Sources

- The power of insight
- Different trusted sources; what to do?
- The 4 key central systems within ITPfM

Chapter 5 Creation of Central Cost System

Chapter 6 Monitoring results

Chapter 7 Start the Improvement & Cost reduction process

Chapter 8 Key benefits of ITPfM

Conclusion

Part 4 Appendix

ITPfM Quick Self-Assessment Results

Index of Topics

About the Author

Part 1 Introduction to ITPfM

The first part of this book is an introduction to the integral ITPfM methodology and the growth of IT costs in organizations resulting in a loss of control on its costs. It also contains a *Quick Self-Assessment* which will provide a (high level) indication of how much control your organization has on IT costs which is reflected in the *ITPfM Cost Control Quadrant.*

ITPfM Integral IT Portfolio Management

Worldwide new applications are developed and released every day. Each day we can do things faster, more efficient and where-ever we want to do it. We can take pictures, while paying for a souvenir in China and inform our friends how lunch looked like in that nice restaurant you just visited. Our IT technology is developing faster than the speed of light it looks like and ……. so do our IT costs!

In organizations, all processes are one way or another supported by IT systems, making an order, calling a customer, producing a piece of hardware, cleaning the office……. all our work is captured in IT systems. Vendors of IT systems are keen to inform us about their latest technologies and applications that make our lives even more easy than they already are and by using it, we always seem to be able to reduce our costs. Cost minded as we always are; this is music to our ears so we eagerly will try to see how the latest software will deliver what was promised.

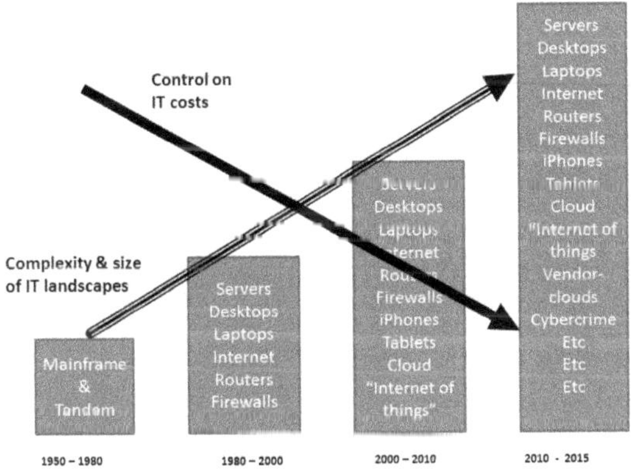

Figure 1 –Graph of growth in IT complexity & costs vs control on IT

We hire armies full of external consultants/experts that will help us understanding all the possibilities this new IT solutions will provide us with and get the maximum out of it. No requirement of an organization is crazy enough, IT systems can deliver it!

That all sounds very good and many companies have really made a difference in the market because of that, but what is always (and I repeat always) forgotten, is to check if all the promises of cost reduction are actually fulfilled. But on the other side do these nice looking applications and systems need faster machines to run on and many times the software license structure is either not clear enough or very short term oriented.

And now a new boost is coming with BIG DATA in THE CLOUD!!!

In other words, IT is growing fast and so do our IT costs! Figure 1 provides an insight of how IT capabilities grow, together with the costs versus the control we have on IT and its costs. With this fast changing and growing of IT landscapes it becomes essential to have a clear vision of what the IT landscape exactly (so not roughly) consists of, how much value it actually brings and how much that actually costs.

With already several IT management models and methodologies in place, the ITPfM methodology does not pretend to bring a new magic model in the world that will have, with a simple push on the button, all your IT costs are under control. What it will do, is outline what has to be done in order to get a clear picture of your IT landscape, how much value it actually brings you and how much it actually costs. It is an integral model in the sense that it will combine different IT management models into a single model that provides a single view on IT within an organization. It consists therefore of all components that one way or another are impacted by IT costs. Smaller companies will find it easier to go through all the steps simply because their organizations have in many cases clear accountabilities for certain IT costs and have short communication lines between them.

Larger organizations will be faced with multiple accountable parties for a single piece of IT equipment and a lot more communication lines between all these parties. The ITPfM methodology applies to both type of organizations; but the larger organizations will need to put significant more effort in making things clear and will gain more out of it as well.

In any case; as ITPfM is an Integral methodology, the roll out needs the endorsement at the highest level in the organization. Because of the potential significant effort that needs to be done to get things clear; you need to avoid political games and traps that frustrate the roll-out process. You will read more about that later in this book

ITPfM – Quick Self-assessment

How much control do you have on your IT expenses?

Before you read further in this book, I advise you to do the *ITPfM Quick Self-Assessment* which will provide you with an initial snapshot to what extend your organization has control over the IT costs and expenses. The ITPfM Quick Self-Assessment below is a questionnaire which contains 10 questions.

Nr	Question	Answer
1	How many employees are employed within your organization?	o < 50 o 50-250 o 250 – 500 o > 500
2	How many employees are employed within IT within your organization	o < 50 o 50-250 o 250 – 500 o > 500
3	How would you rate the size of your total IT landscape	o Almost no IT o Small o Medium o Large
4	What is the percentage of total IT cost vs total costs within your organization?	o <10% o 10% – 30% o 30% - 60% o 60%
5	Are all IT budgets managed centrally within your organization?	o Yes o No
6	Are there many major IT projects taking place in your organization?	o Yes o No
7	Are there many changes in the market your organization participates in?	o Yes o No
8	Are you able to determine how many servers your IT landscape contains within 3 days?	o Yes o No
9	Does your Enterprise IT landscape contain multiple ERP systems (of different vendors)?	o Yes o No
10	Does your Enterprise IT landscape contain different versions of Microsoft (or related software packages) for day-to-day business?	o Yes o No

Table 1 – ITPfM Quick Self-Assessment ©

Please answer the questions as honest as possible (otherwise there will no learning taking place) in the answer boxes on the right. Once you have done the assessment you can go to appendix 1 at the end of this book to verify your results. Once you're done you can continue with the following chapters, with the right mindset on costs!

ITPfM - Cost Control Quadrant

To give you an indication of how much control your organization has on IT costs and expenses you can project your results of the ITPFM Self-Assessment in the *ITPfM - Cost Control Quadrant* © (figure 2) below which presents the two key factors (or variables) that influence the IT expenses in an organization, which are:

1. Size of IT landscape and
2. Complexity of the IT landscape.

Both factors are explained in more detail later in this chapter, but these 2 factors often have the main influence on the control on IT costs. Although these are the main two factors of importance; there are off course also other factors that influence the control on IT costs, depending on the type of organization and sometimes even the business or market you are in. When doing a deeper assessment please ensure these factors are captured adequately to get the right picture. If your organization scores high in both key factors there are strong indications that there is less control on IT costs and expenses than desired. If your score is low on both there is a big chance that you have your IT costs and expenses quite under control, nothing more. Considering that all IT landscapes evolve over time anyway the optimum area is right in the middle, covering all areas in the ITPfM Cost Control Quadrant.

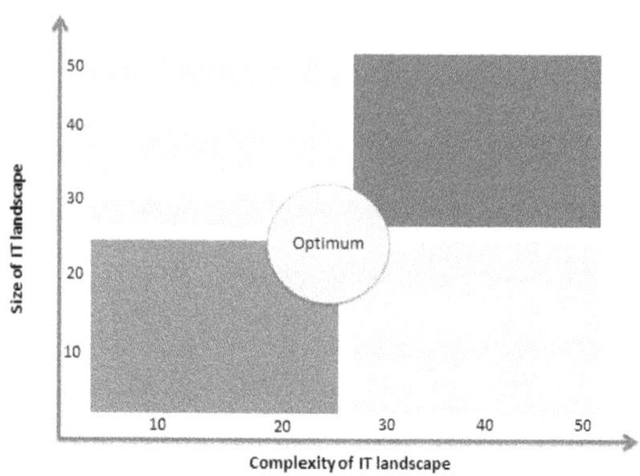

Figure 2 –ITPfM Cost Control Quadrant ©

Factor 1: Size of IT landscape

The size of the IT landscape is a key indicator for control on costs, simply because the more different types of components an IT landscape contains, the more effort is needed to keep control over all of them. Everybody understands this naturally, but it is sometimes striking to see how many organizations think they have control over all their components within their IT landscape while all they have at best is only a vague idea about the 10 most expensive components. It requires solid financial and operational discipline to capture and monitor all relevant financial data about all your IT components; no matter how insignificant they appear at first. Think for example about data storage; which costs nowadays around $10,- per Giga-bite per month (off course this number depends on where the data is stored). In principle not a very interesting topic, until you realize that within your organization Tera bites of data are stored (an in many cases 50% of the stored data is either redundant or out dated!).

We all know that a lot of small items make one big item but practice is that when the number of components become too much (as this can vary per organization) IT cost management gets less emphasis rather than more.

Factor 2: Complexity of IT landscape

Next to the size of the landscape does the complexity of the landscape determine for a big part the level of control on IT costs. Complexity in IT can be caused by different reasons; for example a lot of different technologies applied in the landscape or difficult/ a high number of interfaces between different systems in the landscape, or just complicated solutions are applied, etc. It is important to verify how your organization scores on this factor in the *ITPfM Quick Self-Assessment* as the simple rule applies, "simplicity is cheaper than complexity".

Note: The *ITPfM Quick Self-Assessment* provides you with a high level indication of how much control your organization has on its IT costs and provides an indication to reduce complexity and gain more insight. It is not a deep analysis of all possible influences on IT costs, but it will clearly point out if you are in the "red zone" which means that you have little to no real control over your IT costs or if your organization has at least some control on it which are the yellow areas.

If your initial results are pointing to the top-right area in the "***Red Zone***" (for example in the case that your overall IT costs are significant and rising fast without knowing the causing factor; or in case a vendor files a dispute of significant size for not paying agreed license fees) I advise you to immediately organize a meeting with the senior leadership in your organization to start making a plan to get control on IT costs back. If you score in the ***"Yellow Zones"***, most likely you have some form of control on your IT costs but could be better. If your score is already in the ***"Green Zone"***, CONGRATULATIONS; your organization already seems to have clear control on the IT expenses. You can read further on how ITPfM works, but maybe you would like to pass this book to someone you know can use it better.

As mentioned above is the ITPfM Quick Self-Assessment a very arbitrary assessment which is added to this book to create a sense of awareness on the subject of IT Value and Costs, so you get the right mindset. There are multiple factors that determine the control on IT costs and expenses as you will read later on in this book, so it will just provide you with an indication, based on two key factors of influence. It is therefore in no means a scientific proven method to determine where exactly IT costs are not in control and shouldn't be used for Business Cases to start using ITPfM. In case your organization starts seeing the need for it based on the assessment, a deeper analysis needs to be performed to determine the actual factors that influence the control on IT costs. Off course does the ITPfM methodology assist in getting this insight and can be used as a guide to get control.

Summary of part 1

In this section of the book you have read about the increase of IT spending worldwide for different reasons, but always resulting in less control on IT costs and expenses within organizations. In addition you have read about the *ITPfM Quick Self-Assessment*; which I strongly advise you to do before reading further in this book, and the *ITPfM - Cost Control Quadrant* in which you can see how your organization scores in IT cost control. The next part of the book is about the theory/methodology of ITPfM and the Integral *ITPfM Value/Cost model.*

Part 2 ITPfM Methodology

The theory

This second part of the book contains the theory behind the ITPFM methodology and more specific the *ITPfM Integrated Value/Cost model,* which is a graphical representation of the ITPFM methodology. Already at the beginning of this century (2003) authors like Nicolas Carr created the foundation for a more integral view on IT costs, but so far only a few organizations adopted this way of managing IT. The mainstream focus has so far been on IT management models that focus on only a part of the IT process and have been adopted by the larger organizations accordingly. In many cases lies the focus on new product and service development (projects - especially in new or fast growing companies) or it is too narrow focused (different IT teams supporting only a part of an organization). *The integrated ITPfM Value/Cost Model* is a model that considers all aspects of IT across all departments of an organization including all IT related teams (areas; planning, project, support, procurement/ vendor) to create an integrated view on all aspects of IT. When reading the theory you will notice that parts of it might already be in place within your organization (although it might be called different) and that other parts still seem to be missing.

One important note before going to the next chapter; It's important to stress that the *ITPfM Integrated Value/Cost model* and related graphs are tools to get insight in IT costs and the value IT brings. It does make use of (and refers to) a collection of already existing models and best practices that focus on specific areas. The aim of the ITPfM methodology is to provide total insight in all aspects of IT within your organization and its related costs and to take action on controlling these costs. For each of the identified blocks in the *ITPfM Quadrant*, different cost management models can be used.

Chapter 1 Integrated ITPfM Value/Cost model

In this chapter the *ITPfM Integrated Value/Cost Model* © will be described together with its key areas of importance called the *ITPfM Quadrant* and the *ITPfM blocks* in it. The ITPfM Integrated Value/Cost model represents the integral view of IT within any part of your organization and contains 2 key focus areas:

1. **Value** of the IT System/component to a business process or function.
2. **Costs** of the IT System/component in total (Total Cost of Ownership)

One of the key ideas behind this model is that IT always must have a reason to exist within an organization by adding value to one, or more, business processes, which justifies the investment or the running costs of IT. Like any business process or function adds value to either a customer (product or service) or other part of the organization, IT must also be seen as a value adding entity within an organization, like a hammer adds value to a craftsman and good calculator to an accountant.

The determination of the value of an IT system (or IT portfolio) is in many organizations not easily done and therefore IT is accepted more as a cost center which just will cost a certain amount of money each year and as long if it doesn't hit the agreed budget ceiling that was made for it, we accept these expenses.

This however is NOT the right way to look at IT. Instead IT must always be viewed as tooling that will make your business or function run cheaper or grow. In other words there must always be a balance between the costs of an IT system and the value it provides to the user/owner of it. In figure 3 below you'll find a graphical representation of the Integral ITPfM Value/Cost Model. In there you will see a number of Cost/Value symbols on key interaction places.

ITPfM Integrated Value/Cost Model

In figure 3 the graphical representation of the ITPfM Integrated Value/Cost model (ITPFM Integrated V/C model) is captured. In the rest of this chapter all components are described in more detail.

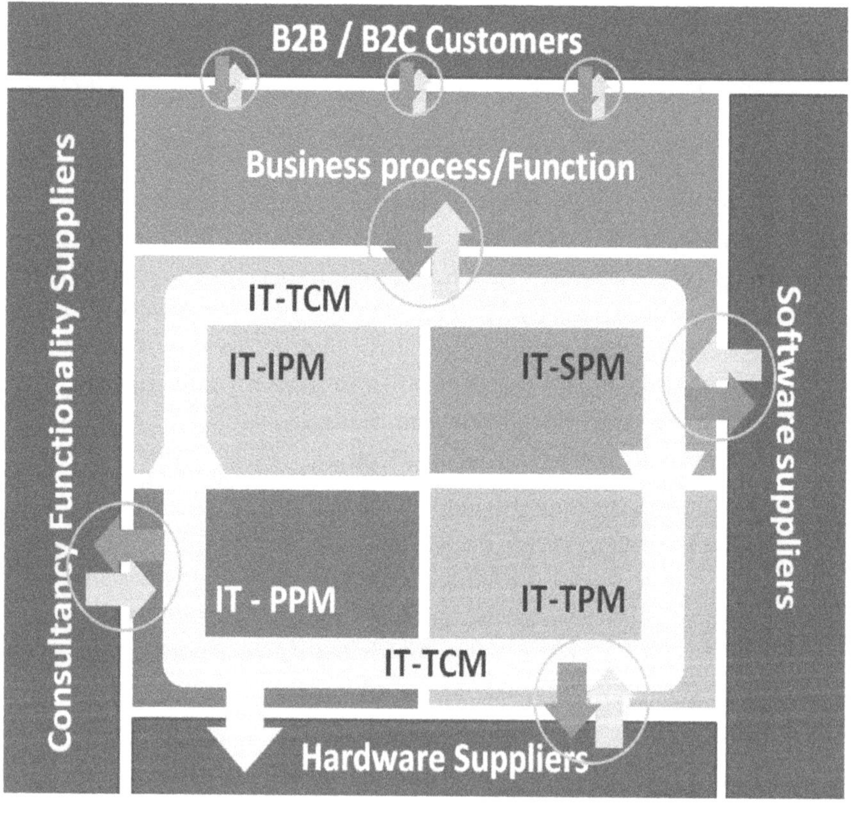

Figure 3 – Integral ITPfM Value/Cost Model ©

Business process or function

The central part of the *Integral ITPfM Value/Cost Model* is the **Business Process or Function**; which is (are) in short the core element(s) of any organization, because these are the places where the value towards customers is actually created and payment is received accordingly. All related IT systems, processes and components that support this business process/function are grouped in a portfolio of IT systems or in other words an ***IT Portfolio***. As there are several business processes or functions in an organization, there will also be several IT Portfolios identified in an organization. These IT Portfolios are the other core part of the ITPfM Integrated V/C model. These IT portfolios are represented in the *ITPfM Quadrant* © which contains the following five *ITPfM Quadrant Blocks* © listed below.

- **IT-IPM: IT Investment Portfolio Management**
- **IT-PPM: IT Project Portfolio Management**
- **IT-SPM: IT-System Portfolio Management**
- **IT-TPM: IT-Technology Portfolio Management**
- **IT-TCM: IT-Total Cost Management**

Each of these ITPfM Quadrants Blocks interact with its environment based on Value and Costs; for simplicity purposes I have selected the specific environmental entities below because in my experience these are the largest environmental elements that influence an IT system but there are off course many other environmental elements which may apply to your organization.

- Consultancy Functionality Suppliers
- Software Suppliers and Hardware Suppliers

The IT portfolio on one hand adds value to the related Business Process/function and in return receives a money/budget for it to operate and when needed to improve, replace and update. (E.g. a mixing machine in a bakery; which saves the baker significant time (and effort) and therefore represents a certain value).

In addition, does the IT portfolio spend money on resources (people, hard and software) either within your organization or outside your organization (suppliers, contracting agencies etc). For each ITPfM Quadrant Block within the IT portfolio the Value/Cost tradeoff must take place on a regular basis; at least once a year. In this review not only the project expenses should be reviewed but also (or especially) the R&M costs and expenses, which are often the hardest to challenge as many IT components and services are embedded in commercial and legally binding contracts.

ITPfM IT Value Model

Next to cost insight, is another important part of the ITPfM methodology the determination what value an IT system (or group of systems/IT portfolio) adds to a business process, which can/must be compared to the costs related to the IT system/IT portfolio in a *Value/Cost trade-off* © (represented by the symbol). The determination the value IT adds to an organization can be (and is) done in many different ways, but in many cases it's done in the form of a Business Case mostly in the situation that new functionality or hardware is considered (as part of an IT project roll-out). There are, however, more situations in which the value of IT needs to be determined and can be grouped in the listed cases below (but off course many others can be considered as well):

- **Automation of a business process**/manual work (IT replaces other elements in Business process; like labor)
- Opportunity to **improve a business process**/function (Efficiency by using IT to do more or faster)
- Fulfilment of a **Legal Requirement** (License to operate)

- **Update** current (old) system with a faster (new) system (Life Cycle)

For each of these cases an analyst compares the current situation with the new situation to justify the expenses needed to make the related change.

In any case, when discussing value of IT, it must always be reflected back to the added value it provides towards the supported Business Process/Function. In other words, <u>the value of an IT system or IT portfolio can only be determined using the assumption that IT is one of the costs elements of a Business Process</u>. Let's for example look at the added value of IT in the production of shoes. As we know, any business process can be described in a "*box model*"; in which a number of input elements results in a desired output. In a simplified example of making shoes, is the result of the business process the number of finished and good quality shoes.

The input elements for making shoes are then for example (but not exclusive):

- Raw material (leather, strings and plastic)
- Cutting Machine
- Sewing machine
- Energy
- Labor (to manage the production process)

In this situation there is no IT system yet so IT doesn't add value to this process. But if we automate the production process by replacing the labor part by a computer that manages the cutting and sewing machine, this could result in a cheaper way to make the shoes. This is a typical investment decision; which is the basis for many IT Automation project proposals. However, once the automation is done (and IT is a cost component of the production process) other type of decision making must take place, e.g. efficiency. If efficiency is made due to faster computers that can optimize the production process further and or make more shoes; there can still be made a case to buy the faster computers as long as we can measure the positive effect on the production process by looking at the output of it (the shoes).

This is in the *ITPfM Value model* called **BCc: Business Capability (Current).**

So far the determination of value of an IT system has been relatively simple. It becomes a lot more difficult if you have IT systems supporting business processes or functions that don't directly add value or don't have clear output units like shoes. Examples are IT system for HR or Legal Departments or Management Information etc. How do you determine the value of the supporting IT systems for these business processes or functions?

The first step should always be the question: are there concrete measurable output (units or effect) that can be measured? For example a number of reports produced by a MI system or legal documents produced by a legal support system, these are clear measureable units to which cost can be allocated. The total costs for the creation of these output units can then be divided by the totally produced output units. This will at least will give you a clear picture of how much each produced unit actually costs which can then be used to determine if that is in line with your expectations or if they are similar to the ones created in other (peer) companies (when using bench marking). This output can then also be captured as **BCc: Business Capability (Current).**

The ITPfM Value Model furthermore identifies the following value adding elements or variables.

L+: Legal requirement fulfilment by IT (added value)

I+: Increase Business Capability due to IT (added value)

E+: Business Process Efficiency due to IT (added value)

With BCc: Business Capability (current) being the current value and the **BCo: Business Capability (Optimized)** the optimized value the following formula to determine the value increase made by IT can be used;

BCo = BBc + E + I + L

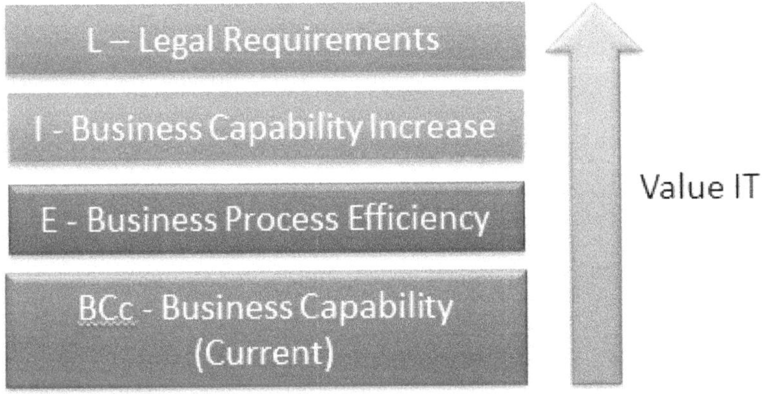

Figure 4 – Simple ITPfM Value Model ©

The above simple ITPfM Value Model (presented in figure 4) provides a simplistic but effective framework to determine the value IT systems provide to any business model and should be used as such, but there are situations that other factors are determining the value which of course than should be added to the above model. Figure 5 below shows the *Detailed ITPFM Value Model ©* in which on more detail the different value adding elements are captured, without losing sight of the essence when determining the value of an IT system or portfolio.

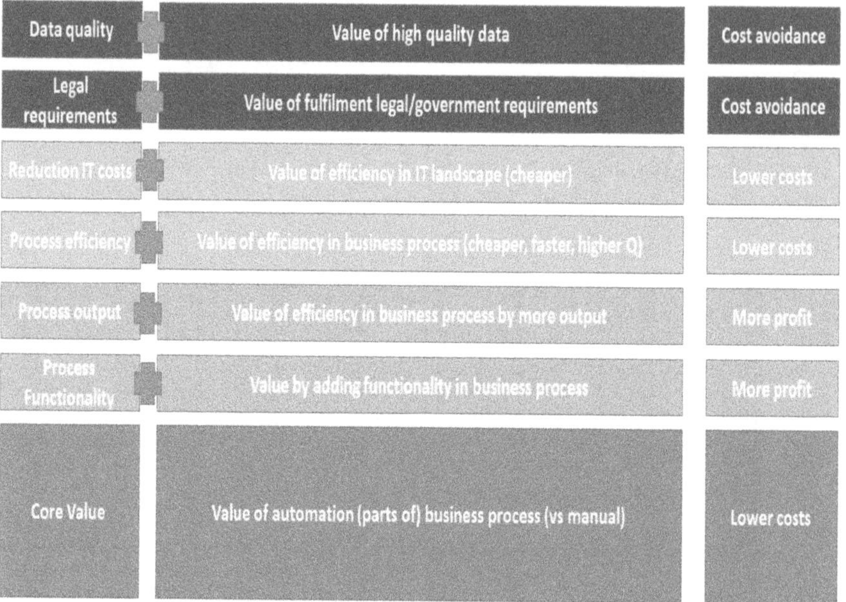

Figure 5 – Detailed ITPfM Value Model ©

ITPfM Quadrant & IT portfolio

As mentioned before does the ITPfM methodology considers IT systems to be supporting a specific business process or function. The total of (related) IT systems that support an identified business process or function is called an **IT portfolio**. *The ITPfM Quadrant* focusses on how IT systems are managed within an IT portfolio. The ITPfM Quadrant consists of 4 key area's within IT that naturally work together, called *ITPfM Quadrant Blocks* ©, and which have on one side a specific value adding function and on the other side spend cost. The 5th element of the ITPfM quadrant connects the other blocks from a cost perspective which can be seen as a flow of cash through the IT portfolio towards the supplying entities. Figure 6 provides a zoom into the core of the Integral ITPfM Value/Cost model; *the ITPfM Quadrant©*.

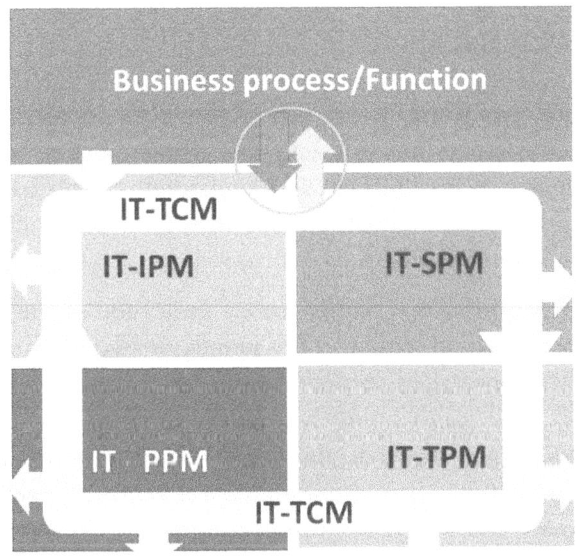

Figure 6 –ITPfM Quadrant ©

In short does the **IT-IPM block** manage the interface between the Business/function and the IT portfolio and manages the IT portfolio budget. The **IT-SPM** block provides the IT systems and services to the business/function, where the **IT-TPM** block ensures all core IT components are running the best way possible in the short and long term. The **IT-PPM** Block is the area where new functionality is added to the current IT portfolio. All Blocks interact with each other in a natural working unit and interact with element within their environment. The **IT-TCM** Block connects all other ITPFM blocks.

In most organizations at least the following two core IT related departments are already working:

- **IT Operations department**; the team/department that runs the Operational IT environments (IT-SPM Block).
- **IT projects department**; the team/department that runs IT projects in Development and Test environments (IT-PPM Block).

In smaller organizations even these two core departments could have been merged into one single IT department or team. For these organizations ITPfM will be relatively simple to implement because all IT related costs should already be pretty clear and only fine-tuning can help to get more grip on IT and IT costs.

Larger organizations typically have a multitude of the above departments added with an IT/Finance or budget function, in many occasions called something similar as Business Interface. In any case; as we go through them in the remainder of this chapter, please keep track of where the ITPfM blocks are situated within your organization. But before we start it's important to first describe the receiving part of the Integral ITPfM Value/Cost model; the Business Process/Function.

ITPfM Quadrant & Blocks

IT-IPM Investment Portfolio Management

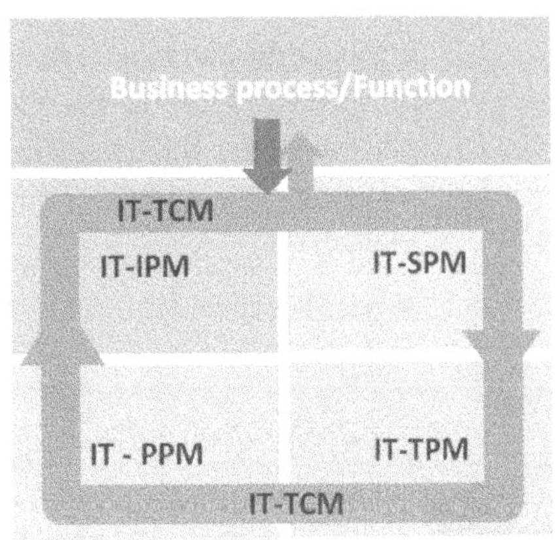

We start with the IT-IPM Block, also called Investment Portfolio Management. This is the area in which the relationships with the Business Process/function is managed and where the Value and Costs of the IT portfolio is determined and monitored. Also the IT Portfolio budgets are managed centrally in this Block. The key purpose of this Block is therefore threefold:

1) Ensure the right business priorities and strategy is translated into technical capabilities, represented in an overall IT investment plan (focused on business outcome)
2) Ensure (accountable for) stable operations and project execution for supported business process/portfolio
3) Ensure the different ITPfM Blocks have enough budget for execution and monitor expenses
4) Evaluate Business Value and execute Business cases for improvement/renewal/new functionality

The IT-IPM Block is typically located in an organization unit/function that is either within the Business/Function itself or closely related to it. It contains activities that are both operational and strategic, but always with the Business processes in mind. Top priority should be stable business operations/processes and as such the people working in this Block work close together with the other Blocks of Support (operations) and Projects.

In many cases will the IT organization remain to be managed based on budgets? Therefore this Block manages the agreed budgets and tracks spending against it in all the other Blocks. As people working in this Block also work close together with the people in the business/function; they are the ones that are responsible for the execution of Business cases and initiation of projects.

Typical activities that are done in this Block are:

- Financial IT Planning creation and monitor
- Business Roadmaps creation and maintain
- Business cases creation and review
- IT scenario planning
- Value/Cost trade offs
- Benchmarking with peer companies
- Relations with market/suppliers

Again all these activities might not be organized within a single role or team, but they are already done. The key is to spot these activities and try to combine them (if needed virtually) to ensure these activities are connected with each other.

IT-SPM System Portfolio Management

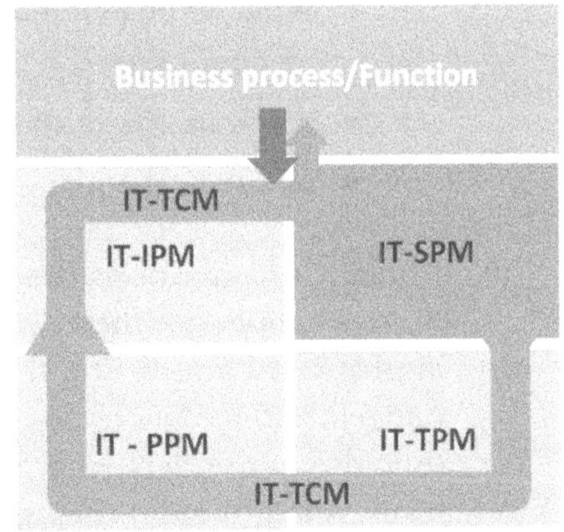

IT System Portfolio Management is the IT area that relates best to the IT operations department of an organization. In this ITPfM Block all technical knowledge is available which is applied to operate the IT infrastructure/landscape. In this area typically are support teams (1st and 2nd line), but also the competence centers, technology architects and product/service managers responsible for the introduction of new products and services and maintenance through their life cycle. The key purpose of this Block is to ensure the IT production environment is running stable at the best possible price for the supported business process/function. The key elements in this area are:

- Ensure operational stability and reliability of the IT systems in the IT landscape
- Ensure a proper IT support structure is in place that can receive and process incoming issues. (like 1st and 2nd line support)
- Ensure all IT systems/components are running licensed and with an adequate capacity
- Monitor running costs of IT landscape (intern or extern).

When it comes to cost control within this area the Total Costs per System are of interest. To be able to do that they need full insight in:

- Which technologies are running in the production environments?

- What is the lifespan/life cycle of these technologies?
- What is the patching/upgrade strategy for these technologies?
- What are the costs for these technologies?
- What are the planned business driven changes?

In many organizations the above information (or at least a basis of it) is simply not there. Especially in larger organizations, both in profit and non-profit, the IT departments are run based on budgets and budget cycles with the sole aim to not overspend (but also not underspend) on the planned budget. The logical result is that there is then no need for more insight into IT components and the related costs. Reducing IT costs or making good business cases for replacing systems or applications is very difficult and in many cases based on incorrect financial data. Studies on why projects fail, published over the years by leading consulting agencies like Mckinsey, Oxford and KPMG indicated that, next to other factors, one of the key reasons for failure is incorrect benefit projection (incorrect data) and failure to measure benefits at all (no correct data at all!!!). But also in case of cost reduction activities it's not possible to get many results if you don't even know how expensive your current systems actually cost. In chapter 3 more detail is given on this topic and how you can get more grip on it. For a good running ITPfM based IT organization it is essential to have detailed clarity on at least the following core elements of your IT landscape:

- Number of servers and which Operation systems is running on it
- Actual costs per server (and licenses fees)
- Number of databases
- Number of middleware components
- Actual costs per component (and license fees)
- Actual costs of IT staff

In many cases, especially in larger organizations, different IT systems are running on the same or similar IT platforms. When applying the ITPfM methodology it is important to ensure that these Blocks for all IT portfolios are closely connected to a central technology team. This will ensure the integral view remains intact and double work and sub optimization is avoided.

IT-TPM Technology Portfolio Management

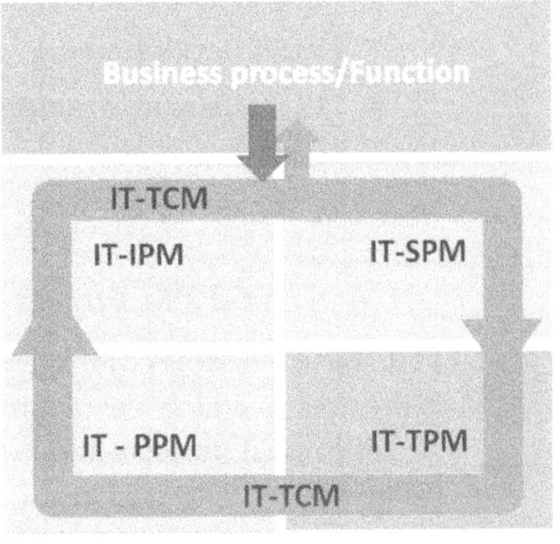

IT Technology Portfolio Management is the Block in which the planning of all systems/applications within the IT portfolio is managed that are running in the IT landscape and their underlying technologies. Because the users working in the Business/Function are the users of the IT systems their "view" on the IT landscape is often only the applications and systems they actually use. It is therefore important to ensure that Total Cost of Ownership per System or application is known as this in many business cases this will be used as a trade-off entity. In addition does this Block also focus on the bigger cost picture of the entire IT portfolio.

Within this Block also the roadmap and life cycles of the Systems/ Applications are managed; which should be aligned with the Business roadmap lined out by the business/function. This means that within this block the future of all applications and their components in the landscape are periodically assessed on Value/Cost but also on supportability. Each vendor of an IT component (both hard and software) keep working to improve their products and make new versions or releases of them. Because all of these new versions have a limited lifespan and the related vendor support for it, it is very important to ensure your IT landscape components the Systems/Applications make use of are evergreen or at least have the vendor support. Also new IT capability or business requirements are managed in this area, which are included in the multi-year portfolio or application roadmaps and planning. Key activities in this area are typically:

- Creation and maintenance of Portfolio roadmaps and system roadmaps
- Architect of landscape and meeting with vendors on latest developments
- Participate in Business cases/reviews and cost reduction initiatives

IT-PPM Project Portfolio Management

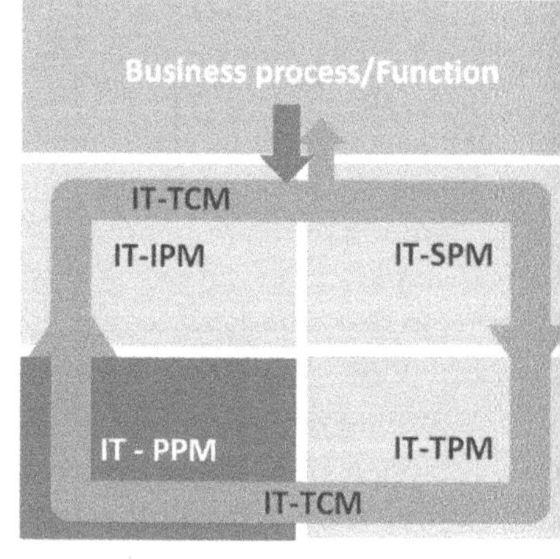

IT Project Portfolio Management is the area in which the planned and approved projects and programs are delivered and managed.

This is perhaps the most common known & understood area that is linked with the term IT portfolio management and in many organizations it is already called like that. It always is related to a number of (IT) projects that are managed as a portfolio or program.

ITPfM does also include the Project Portfolio Management function and activities, but only as a part (block) of the integral IT landscape. This makes it different than most of the current views on IT Portfolio management, but in essence its focus and activities of this Block are what is already considered part of IT portfolio management. There are already many different models and supporting software for this ITPfM block in place in the market so I will not spend too much time on it, but only list the key activities in this area.

- Participation in Business Cases and reviews
- Initiation and Execution of IT projects and programs
- Meeting with vendors and functional consultancy agencies
- Change Management in Business/Function

Important to mention here as well is that in order to effectively roll-out projects and programs; it is essential that good communication with the other ITPfM blocks within the IT portfolio is done; specially with the IT-ITM block which is responsible for the IT delivery towards the business process/function.

IT-TCM Total Cost Management

IT Total Cost Management is the central block of the ITPfM Integral Value/Cost model in which all financial aspects of the different ITPfM blocks come together in a single and transparent way. It's in other words the heart of the ITPfM cost model.

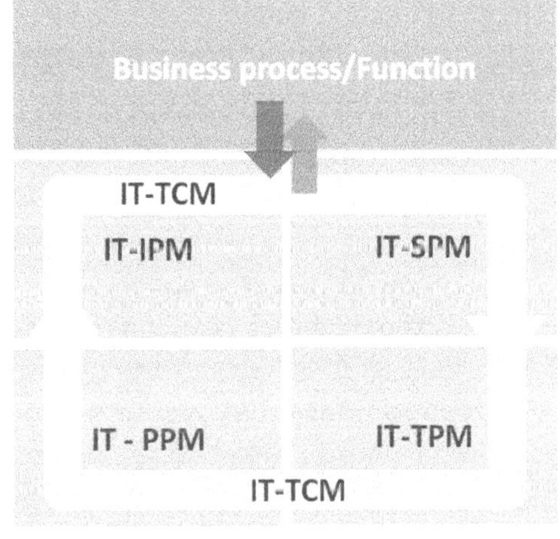

To ensure total and integral control on cost in an organzation, it is very important to have a single central system in which all cost elements are captured and monitored; that acts as the **single truth** on costs. In addition there should be a central ITPfM Cost Management Team in an organization that manages, amoung other things, this central cost management system. This will enable the management team of an organization to analyse the IT costs data across all the the different IT Portfolio's which enables them to make cross portfolio decisions; for example on platform level (should we use windows or linux).

Within each IT portfolio all costs must be administered adequately and must be transparent for all participants in the central Total Cost Management system. This is in many cases easier said that actually done, especially in larger organizations, where costs are captured in different ways, in different systems and often with different cost variables. So when considering the roll out of the ITPfM methodology in your organization, sufficient time and effort must be reserved for getting this right.

With a strong and solid IT-TCM block the other ITPfM blocks will be enabled to perform their activities right and efficient as everybody talks about the same costs in the same language. For the management team it will prove to be a very valuable source of information.

How the different ITPfM Quadrant Blocks work together

All ITPfM blocks work on one hand on very specific activities and responsibilities related to the Block, but on the other hand they will work close together with the other blocks in the ITPfM Quadrant to ensure a solid and strong IT portfolio supports the related Business Process/Function. How people working in the different blocks can and should work together will be described in part 3. When starting to use the ITPfM methodology you will soon notice that in your organization there is an emphasis on one (or two) ITPfM blocks; which makes each ITPfM roll-out unique. Although all ITPfM blocks perform a key role in the total model; it will off course be beneficial to focus on the key blocks for your own organization.

Summary of part 2

In this section of the book you have read about the theory of the ITPfM Integrated Value/Cost Model and the ITPfM Quadrant and Blocks. It's important to understand that ITPfM is an integral model that manages all aspects of IT within an organization. Each Block represents in many cases an organizational/business unit or team that is responsible for the delivery of that particular part of IT. The alignment of the different Building Blocks/teams within a specific portfolio with the business process its supports is a key enabler for success. In many cases this results in the formation of teams working together in a Natural Way, in which all key players are represented and jointly work on solutions or costs reductions within that specific portfolio.

Part 3 ITPfM – Introduction and Roll out

Introduction and Roll out in organizations

In this section of the book you will read about how ITPfM can be rolled out in your own organization. It's based on best practices of companies that have already successfully introduced ITPfM, and as such could be helpful for introducing ITPfM within your organization. What always must be kept in mind is that each organization has its own characteristics so therefore always ensure the advice that is written down in this part of the book make sense. There are however a number of key rules which apply across all types of organizations so should be followed for a successful introduction and roll out of ITPfM.

Chapter 2 Is your organization ready?

To verify if your organization is ready to start with the introduction of the ITPfM methodology, there are a number of factors that need to be considered first. As a roll out of ITPfM will have significant impact on the current organizational structure and ways of working, it's advised to first do a check how ready your organization actually is for a significant change, as this will increase significantly the chances for a successful introduction of ITPfM.

Factor 1: Leadership endorsement and right governance

To start with the most important success factor; for each initiative that is important in an organization it's essential that the leadership team not only agrees that the change is important, but that it also endorse it. There is an important difference between these two and they become especially visible when issues arise during the roll out of any initiative. As mentioned in part 2 of this book can the roll out of the ITPfM methodology result in a major change in an organization resulting in a significant impact on the current way of working of people and departments. Without wanting to go into much detail about the importance of good Change Management practices, I do want to stress that in case issues arise or conflicting views stop the progress of the introduction of ITPfM, the leaders of the organization must emphasize the importance of having the total control on IT costs and therefore fully supports and endorses the required changes. In many larger organizations the so called "Ivory towers" already block any form of real integration; the integration of the whole IT organization into a single managed organization will result in less power for the teams in these ivory towers. It's therefore essential to have clear mandate of the leadership for the ITPfM roll out teams. In case of issues escalation to senior levels can quickly resolve any hurdle or difficulty that is met. If there is no endorsement from the leadership of an organization the chances for a successful roll out of ITPfM are reduced significantly. In addition it's very likely that the formation of a portfolio based IT organization will result in organizational changes. The leadership of the organization must create the proper guidelines of how the new organizational structure must look like.

Factor 2: Size of organization

The second most important factor for a successful introduction of ITPfM in an organization is the size of the organization. Without wanting to make this factor too academic as well, there have been a significant number of studies done on the success of introducing changes in large organizations versus small organizations. Most of them conclude that because smaller companies have shorter communication lines and less management layers the leaders of such organizations are a lot better able to initiate and establish changes rather than the larger organizations that, by design, have many more management layers and communication lines and many times also have a certain *corporate culture* in which changes are handled a certain way. ITPfM can successfully be rolled out in every organization, either large or small, but the "Change Effort" will be significantly higher in larger organizations than in smaller ones. In a smaller organization perhaps a single person could manage the introduction of the ITPfM methodology with a small team of people in the different Blocks. In larger organization it will most likely require a program with a number of related change projects, each with their own project team and champions in the different business units or functions. It will also require an integral view across the entire organization that in large organizations is more difficult (but definitely not impossible) than smaller organizations. The key to success for this factor is to ensure that on the appropriate management level this integral view on IT is made and kept; most of times done by a central change team. This team will be the central point for all change teams in the different parts of the organization.

Factor 3: Size of IT within the organization

I have added the size of the IT landscape(s) within an organization as a separate factor (next to just the size of an organization), because the size of an IT landscape and supporting organization, in many occasions, gives an indication of how complex the IT landscape is. In chapter 1 you read that over time IT in organizations grew with sometimes the speed of light and in many cases, there were (and still are) different IT departments each managing their own part of the (IT) business on their own specific way. This is most of times done on a decentralized bases; which results that often each part of the organization has its own IT solutions and vendors. Sometimes even for similar processes. The result is then, looking with an integral perspective at the total IT landscape of an organization, a patch work of IT solutions, each growing into a different direction.

The cause of this situation varies per organization. In many cases IT "just developed that way" because IT was managed on a lower (department) level within the organization with the only focus on optimizing that part. Another important reason can be acquisition or merger of companies/organizations where each company has its own different IT infrastructure to support their key business processes.

ITPfM forces organizations to look with integral glasses on to their IT landscape(s) and therefore will show the differences in IT technologies, solutions and applications and in many cases the redundancies are immediately clear. In chapter 5 will be described how to start with this.

Factor 4: Level of insight in total IT costs

The level of insight in IT costs is in many organizations only available in a very aggregated level. Especially in larger organizations IT departments are managed by budgets and as long as all is running below a certain budget all is fine. THIS IS NOT THE RIGHT MINDSET IF YOU WANT TO GET CONTROL OVER IT COSTS!!!

Managing everything based on budgets only, results in little to no focus to reduce costs. The main reason for this is that if you reduce costs you could also reduce the budget, but many managers feel that a reduction in their budget is a reduction of their importance and power. So there is in many occasions no direct incentive to reduce costs, only if it is enforced from above.

This results in the situation that everybody tries to initiate projects that increase the budgets rather than reducing them. There is a lot of focus on the project; it's planning and finances, but always very little on what impact the results of the project have on the supportability of the IT landscape so they forget about a focus on how much the operational costs will be impacted. In other words, organizations in many cases do know, on high level, how much IT costs at the end, but a drill down and justification of IT costs is in many cases simply not possible and therefore not done, resulting that they miss out on major opportunities to reduce IT costs!

For a successful use of ITPfM an organization must have detailed information about all its IT Portfolios, Landscapes, Components and Systems/Applications. Organizations that already have a certain level of cost insight in place are only a few steps away from managing their IT on an integrated way and the resulting ability to reduce costs. Organizations that don't have this insight will first need to start getting it. In the following chapters it will be described how to do that.

Chapter 3 ITPFM Organization

Creation of a single IT organization

In a single phrase is this chapter about the creation of a single integral and aligned IT function within your organization; all IT is managed centrally, there is no room for exceptions and special cases, all IT portfolios are working in similar ways. In order to get to this integral way of working, this chapter outlines the structure that needs to be in place in order to let the ITPFM methodology work smoothly.

Creation of a single IT function

The roll out of ITPfM within any organization starts with the creation of a single (virtual in the beginning if needed) IT function across the entire organization. All existing departments must be relocated and mapped into this single IT organization. For smaller companies this most of times is reorganizing the different IT staff into one (virtual) team; in larger companies this could already mean the first major change/reorganization. The top leadership of your organization must first assign a central change team that will manage this step (and following steps) in the whole organization. All IT teams and departments will be involved in later stages.

During this activity will the central IT team review the current IT organization and make a blueprint to transform it (at least on paper) into a single managed integral IT function across the organization. Preferably is this new integral IT function aligned with the different business processes or functions across the organization and in case of multiple teams working in similar processes across different locations; they must all be (re-)assigned to a single portfolio within the IT function. (If desired in a later stage you could decide to add geometrics in your new IT function). Once the central team is set up and made the blue print for the new integrated IT function the following steps can be made.

The result of this step is an integral IT structure across the organization; with different logical IT portfolios connected to the key business processes in the organization. So there will for example be an IT portfolio supporting the purchasing process, another IT portfolio for the production process and another one for the sales process etc. In addition, depending on the business processes, you can add IT portfolios for functions like HR, finance, legal etc. It's important to have logical groups of IT systems as the basis for the portfolios.

In this step the IT Portfolio managers roles should be formed/created and key managers/staff assigned for each of the 4 ITPfM roles per ITPfM Quadrant Blocks. It is not that important how these roles are named as long as the key responsibilities are in line with the ITPfM Quadrant Blocks the role is connected to. Below are short, high level descriptions of the ITPfM roles and connected responsibilities within each of the ITPfM Quadrant Blocks.

ITPfM Roles within IT Portfolio

IT-IPM: IT Investment Portfolio Manager

The IT-IPM is in principle the interface with the supported business/functions and the overall budget holder of the portfolio. He/she has a small team of Business analysts who work together with the business/function on new projects and to ensure operational stability. In this role are also the Value and Costs trade-offs made together with the business process managers.

IT-PPM: IT Project Portfolio Manager

The IT-PPM is the project/portfolio manager that is responsible for the appropriate execution of all identified IT projects within the portfolio. He/she typically has a team of Project Managers/staff that are delivering projects that were reviewed by the BA's in the IT-IPM block and is also responsible for managing the IT project costs/expenses. This role can also be responsible for the Change and Engagement process towards the end user communities.

IT-TPM: IT Technology Portfolio Manager

The IT-SPM is in principle the Strategy and Planning manager that ensures the current IT portfolio and landscape runs on desired/supported hard and software and is responsible for Integral planning and System Roadmaps. He/She typically has a team of IT analysts that work together with vendors on testing/verifying new solutions. As many times portfolio's run of specific large systems, IT-SPM is in many cases also the linking block with the other blocks.

IT-TPM: IT System Portfolio Manager

The IT-IPM is in principle the Operations manager that ensures the current landscape runs stable and secure and is always available for the end users in the different Business processes or functions. He/she typically has a team of IT support staff (1st and 2nd line) and is also responsible for managing the IT costs/expenses and the monitoring of the Total Cost of Ownership (TCO) of the IT systems and related landscape within the IT portfolio.

IT-TCM: IT-Total Cost Manager

The IT-TCM is in principle the focal point for all cost related matters within the IT portfolio and therefore a key role between the other roles. All roles need to ensure that within their ITPfM Quadrant Block they have all data and costs clear; the IT-TCM will combine all data for the portfolio and ensure the Central Cost Control system is kept up-to-date.

Portfolio teams/ITPfM Teams

Within each portfolio all different ITPfM roles should work together in *Portfolio Teams* or ITPfM teams. These Portfolio Teams will collectively be responsible for the adequate functioning of the IT portfolio. They will already work together in a natural way, but because of common ownership of the IT portfolio, they will be insentivated to work together on common goals. In some organizations these are called Natural Teams others call them Portfolio focus groups of simply portfolio teams. It is not important how it's called, but essential that they work tightly together and meet regularly. In principle is the IT-IPM the ideal virtual Portfolio Team lead, but off course any of the ITPfM roles are able to manage the agenda and team meetings of the Portfolio Teams.

Chapter 4 Introduction of a single truth

Work with trusted Information Sources

To start to get control over your IT costs you first need to know exactly how expensive your IT landscape and all its components are at the moment. Let's call this the creation of a snapshot of your current IT expenses. A good analogy that applies here is what you would do to get control over your expenses privately. When you want to get control over your income and expenses at home you'll first start listing all costs and income elements you can think of and then you find the actual numbers for them, right. Well, the same should be done for all components within your IT landscape. How this works is described in chapter 7; Cost insight – creation of single IT Cost Control System. What we'll discuss in this chapter is the importance of using what we call "Single Truth/ Trusted Sources." *(Definition trusted source: a trusted source is a single source that contains the actual data of a required data requirement).* When we would look for a trusted source for your income; you most likely would go to check your bank statements or, even better, you would go to your monthly pay slip on which your salary (and all its salary components) are outlined. The same goes for trusted sources for costs within your IT department. In many organizations IT costs are not very transparent because the trusted sources are not adequately used or the right people have no access to them. IT costs are often mainly bases on "IT budgets" which are in many cases mainly based on assumptions and planned costs; not actual costs. For example: When you would like to know how much your server park in your IT landscape would cost; you initially would ask the IT manager. If you are lucky he/she knows an average amount per server; based on what he has picked up once when he/she was involved purchasing one. But the reality is EACH SERVER

HAS A DIFFERENT PRICE!!. Like a car, a server can have options that makes it cheaper or more expensive (RAM, Disc size, CPU's etc). So, although an average can be used for budgets; it's hardly a trusted source for your actual IT spending. If you want to know how much your IT landscape actually costs; you need to dive deeper in your landscape than just to know how many servers you have running (although; just try to get that number clear and you'll see that this information is already difficult to get). In any case, if you want to know what exactly you are running and paying for you best can go to the person/department that is responsible for the contracts with the IT vendors and paying the related invoices. Only in the invoices you receive from your vendors; you'll see the actual costs of your IT landscape, so this is a clear example of a trusted source. Before you read further try to find the answer to the following question: who is responsible for the IT contracts and payment for the invoices in your organization? If you know the answer on top of your head; please contact this person today and ask for a specified invoice for all your components in your landscape. If you don't know; please check today who in your organization is the right person. Without this information you will never have a chance of getting grip on your IT expenses. Like in your private situation; if you would like to know how much you spend on power and gas; you would go to check your monthly invoice, right? Trusted sources are a key enabler for getting grip on your IT costs; look for them until you have them!

The power of insight

Once you put yourself to start using trusted sources instead of budgets and spreadsheets; you will soon see that you'll have a lot more detailed information available to you then you realized. Let's again go to your private situation in which you review your gas and power bill. Once you look at the invoice; you will immediately check your monthly consumption and the price per unit, right? You will also spot some costs that don't make immediate sense to you (trust me these costs are listed there!). Supplying companies are by law enforced to give you disclosure on all cost elements of the product/service you buy/pay for. Even on your super market ticket is a lot more information than you would guess, check it out!). Focusing on the details of an invoice triggers at least the following questions (but hopefully more)

"Why am I consuming so much gas or power?"

"Is all that needed/is there room for saving some dollars/Euro's etc)? "

"What are all those additional costs for?"

All questions triggered by looking at an invoice are good questions, because you finally give the invoice the attention that it needs. The same goes for IT invoices for your organization. They will contain all the mandatory information and help you to better understand what IT exactly is running on in your environment and how much that costs you each month (or year). If invoices are a lump sum invoice; you are entitled for a full breakdown of the cost elements below it. Ask your finance department or contract department for a breakdown if that is not initially available. You must ask to the level of understanding that makes sense for you! Specially with automated invoicing; you are seduced not checking your invoice (out of "easiness"), but please take the time to verify what you pay for! I am sure you immediately will spot some costs that you don't recognize. Recent research in shopping behavior of customers in supermarkets shows that only 10% of the people actually checks the bill after paying the invoice, but that at least 15% of the invoices contains a mistake (most of the times in your disadvantage)! Therefore always check your invoice and understand the costs elements and their related costs. I bet you that when you check the invoices charged for your IT landscape you'll spot immediately a number of payments that you don't recognize or even know are incorrect. Challenge them!!

Different trusted sources; what to do?

The larger an organization; the further away you most likely will be from the trusted sources like invoices to IT vendors. You most likely will also be faced with different sources for the same information. Each department has its own spreadsheet for budgets and cost allocation; which makes it difficult to determine what you IT costs actually are. Don't give up here in your search for the true IT costs. Digg deeper into the chain until you come to the cost level that you understand and is in relation with the IT landscape that you are responsible for.

In the next chapter we'll go deeper into what should be done to avoid "multiple truths", the creation of a single source of IT costs/ IT cost management system; the ITPfM Cost Control System.

The 4 key central systems within ITPfM

Central Technology System (CTS) - Integral picture of all IT components

With the Central ITPfM team in place and the IT organization transformed into a Business process/portfolio based structure, with all the ITPfM roles assigned to the right people; the second step can be made; the creation of the integral picture of all IT landscapes within the organization and portfolio's. This is the area where initially all roles will play a major part to get all the relevant data in the central control systems.

The first thing to do is to create a trusted and single source in which all technical and functional IT components is captured; the **Central Technology System (CTS)**. This can maybe be done in a spreadsheet within small companies, but larger companies need a special system for that and there are several systems in the market for this, for example HP Asset Manager.

Then the second major operation starts; all relevant IT staff have to start to register all IT components in their landscape together with all the key information items that are required to manage that those adequately. Examples of IT components are Servers, Databases, Middleware, firewalls, application components, interfaces etc, basically everything that needs maintenance and have a cost related to that. For each of the identified components a large list of attributes must be captured (and maintained) to ensure all data is relevant and up-to-date.

The IT-SPM and his team are responsible for gathering all relevant data to fill the Central Technology System. They work together with vendors support teams to gather all the relevant data and keep it up-to-date.

Central Application System – Integral picture of all IT

Next to the registration of all IT components; it's also essential to capture all the applications that the end-users in the business/function use within the IT portfolio. This is captured in the **Central Application System (CAS)**. This CAS is in principle the basis for capturing how all component registered within the CTS are used by the identified business/function application/systems. In other words, on this application/system level are all underlying components linked. With this set up it is then possible to determine which components are used by with applications; which is essential to know once we start to focus on costs.

It is therefore very important that all applications end users are using are captured in the CAS and there are in principle 2 types of applications/systems.

a) IT support systems; these are the systems the IT function is responsible for in terms of delivery and cost management
b) Business supported systems: these are the systems that third parties manage directly without interference of the IT functions.

The Business Support systems also must be captured in the CAS as that is needed to create a complete integral IT picture. It must also be reviewed why they are managed without involvement of the IT function. There could be strategic reasons for it, but in general terms should the IT function manage all applications/ systems to avoid inefficiencies and increase in costs.

Typical data captured in the CAS are: Unique identifier, name + description of an application/system, version/release, Life cycle status, roll outs/deployments within organization etc.

Central Project System (CPS) Integral picture of all Projects in the IT landscape(s)

This maybe the best kept up-to-date area within your current organization. Because of the temporal nature of projects and a clear cost/benefit case that is made before the projects starts, in many organizations there is already some form of (de)central system(s) in which the key IT project related data is kept, like budget, spend cost to date, planning etc. What is important however is to have an integral view of ALL IT projects within the organization (large and small ones); so some effort might be needed to collect everything in a single central project system (CPS).

There are several vendors that supply CPS systems for organizations. Typical data captured in the CPS are: Unique identifier, name + description of a project, project budget, spending per month, etc.

Central Investment System (CIS) – Integrated picture of Investments

In many organizations the budgets and finances are already well captured in spreadsheets and they are in many cases also already integrated. If this is not the case it is essential to start with this first. There are many different financial applications/systems available in the market. Examples are Exact for small/medium organizations and ERP systems like SAP, Oracle etc for the large organizations.

What is important to have in place is a clear overview of all Investment items projects, upgrades, new legal requirements etc.

Data quality in Central systems

During the implementation of ITPfM in an organization a lot of focus needs to be on getting the trusted sources within the different ITPfM blocks ready with a 100% data quality. Without good quality data in the central systems there is still room for misinterpretation which results in mistrust of the reports that come out of these systems. It is therefore very important to put emphasis on getting the data right in from the start and keep it evergreen once implemented.

It is therefore important to have clear roles & responsibilities defined (like data value owner, data collection owner) together with an embedded process to keep the data clean.

Regular reviews can be done based on the data in the systems in which in depth the ITPfM Natural team works through the different applications and underlying component structures.

Having high quality data in the 4 key ITPfM systems is also important to gain insight on the top management layer of an organization. The next chapter will describe the Central Cost System in the 4 key central systems feed into.

Chapter 5 Creation of Central Cost System

With the creation of the 4 central systems for each of the ITPfM Quadrant Blocks there are 4 single (trusted) sources of information for the different areas within the portfolio, including costs, which will already provide a lot of clarity about IT in your portfolios and good work can already start to improve it. However it is needed to have, in addition, a single source for all IT costs across all portfolios in which the central ITPfM team and the leadership of the organization can create a total picture of all IT portfolios.

As first step of the creation of the CCS, the central ITPfM team needs is to determine, together with the leadership of an organization, what central information needs to be captured in order to make strategic choices about the IT landscape.

Initially the focus will be in capturing and understanding the current integral landscape and the related costs and cash flows. By doing this, almost immediately the large "cost gaps" become already visible. Typical observations that are made by senior IT managers are like the ones below:

> *"Wow, we have 2000 servers running in our organizations; what are they all doing?"*
>
> *"We seem to have 500 servers running in our landscape that nobody seems to use (zombie servers). What is running on these servers?"*
>
> *"The total current IT spent is 50 million higher than we have captured in our financial system; how is that possible?"*

The CCS must interface with all 4 key central ITPfM systems, but also needs to be connected to the payment system to vendors and perhaps there is a need to connect other systems to it to be able to get all the relevant data into the CSS. What is very important to stress is that the data that feeds into this system is all coming from trusted sources and not entered manually or uploaded manually with a spreadsheet. Any manual intervention or upload can degrade the data quality significantly and gives room to have "alternative sources of the truth."

There are a number of CSS type applications available in the market (e.g. Apptio – Accenture), but you can also develop your own. During the selection process of the CSS application it's important that

1) All relevant data can be captured in it and

2) All report requirements are met.

It is good to have the ability to make some additional reporting or interface yourself as during the course of the ITPfM journey you'll realize that your information need will change over time.

In principle should all ITPfM managers have access to the CSS in order to

a) Verify that all data in it is OK and

b) To help them keeping control over the costs of their portfolio's.

With all the high quality data available in the CSS you can start creating a monitor or dashboard across your organization that will in a unified way show the core IT management reports that you wish to focus on. In the next chapter you will find how to start with this.

Chapter 6 Monitoring results

With all your IT components captured in the 4 ITPfM systems/ trusted sources and all IT costs captured into your single CSS system your organization has achieved a major milestone! Congratulations! What you now have captured, in simple terms, is what you actually have (IT components) and how much they costs, in detailed terms. As mentioned before; you must have insight at "invoice/billing" level as that is the level the money concrete leaves your organization.

What you now have to do is monitor the results that come out of your CSS system (are the costs stable, or are there increases) and start making detailed reviews also called "Detailed Analysis Sessions" per IT portfolio to understand in detail what the key IT systems and components are and how much is spent on that. This has to be done by the portfolio teams or natural teams together with the business/function users that make use of the IT portfolio systems and components.

These Detailed Analysis Sessions (DAS) can best be triggered and managed by the central ITPfM team; which works together with the portfolio teams. They are best able to provide a single template of data that needs to be captured and can insure an aligned approach. In addition can the central ITPfM team gain an integral view which is useful when comparing IT technologies between the different IT portfolios.

Keep in mind that the first round of these Detailed Analysis Sessions most likely will have a significant impact on your IT department and the portfolio teams. Although all systems of the ITPfM Quadrant Blocks are in place, there will be issues with data gathering, interpreting the results and creating the desired central view of the portfolio. Important is to have all documentation available for everybody involved in the ITPfM roll out and that it's clear what exactly is expected by when.

Templates are a great help as well as central web sessions with all participants. It is very important that all portfolios are creating the same overview because only then you will be able to start comparing portfolios with each other. If each portfolio still have their unique way of data presentation comparing will be impossible, resulting in wrong results and decisions. Key information elements are (but definitely not a complete list)

- Total number of servers in portfolio
- Total number of Databases in portfolio
- Total number of systems in portfolio
- Total cost per system in portfolio
- Total cost of complete portfolio

Initial insights

When reviewing and analyzing all ITPfM data the different members in the team will without any doubt run into questions and insights. "Why do we have this server" or "why is this database so expensive" or "This server should have been decommissioned already 2 years ago" are typical questions that are asked during these initial Detailed Analysis Sessions and focused effort can be placed on already solving this issues. Like when you have insight on your monthly expenses, you immediately want to stop the subscription (e.g. of a magazine) that you didn't even know you still were paying for and you already made the first steps of reducing your IT costs. Although these Detailed Analysis Sessions do take significant effort, it is advised to do them once a year. Once the first one is done, the 2nd and 3rd one will be a lot easier to do and the central ITPfM team and portfolio teams know how to work with the trusted sources. In the best case the portfolio teams make a regular review themselves to ensure all data is up-to-date and surprises are immediately spotted and actioned.

Chapter 7 Improvement & Cost reduction

With all parts of the ITPfM Methodology working and the monitoring is in place your organization has achieved what it wanted; total insight and control of your IT costs and a clear picture of the value IT provides to the supported Business Processes and Functions! This is the key aim of the ITPfM methodology. Because you are in control, you will at least know how many IT components there are running in your landscape and what they actually cost you per month or year.

Your organization is now ready for the next steps to gain the deeper benefits of the ITPfM methodology. In this book I will, as example, describe a small selection of benefits that every organization should be able to work on and gain at least some benefits from. As mentioned earlier in this book the actual cost reductions will depend greatly on both the size of the organization and the complexity of the landscape.

Upfront advice before taking action on Improvement and Cost take out. Another important factor of influence on the IT landscape is the level of change that is taking place in the IT landscapes. Within each portfolio major projects or even go-lives can take place at the moment ITPfM is rolled out. In these situations; where the Landscape is "fluid" due to all the changes that take place in it, it's recommended not to take out too many components out of the landscape; except if there is clear evidence that the components in question absolutely will not impact the success of an IT project/program go live.

Selection of new IT technology

A clear example in which the benefits of using the ITPfM methodology will become visible is the situation when new IT technology (hardware or software) is considered by an organization. In many cases is this triggered by a sales or account manager of a supplying company or new company; who shows the latest developed IT Technology which makes everything FASTER, SMOOTHER and will provide more BUSINES INSIGHT and… WILL LOWER YOUR COSTS! Sound familiar? When selecting new IT technology it is either "just" an upgrade of your current landscape or a replacement of IT components. It is very important to always verify with at least 2 other vendors that provide similar hard or software what their products are and how much they cost. I trust that the benefit of doing this is clear and also trust that many organizations, including the one you work in, already has this good practice in place.

But now it comes; the key benefit of having ITPfM in place. At the moment the sales/ account manager has done their presentations and maybe even provided a sample of the product for testing, there is the discussion and negotiations about money (initial costs, licenses etc). This is an area where many larger organizations struggle, mainly for the reason that they have a separate procurement team that does the negotiations. The people in this team are without doubt masters in negotiating, but in many cases they are not all that knowledgeable in IT but more importantly they don't have a clear picture of how much a component in the landscape actually costs. So basically in many occasions they are negotiating without a solid basis to compare from. The result is than off course only as good as it sounds without a solid basis and as long as it fits in the related budgets it's considered to be OK. Key problem areas are always: 1) what are the direct costs of the product vs the Run and Maintain costs later in time and 2) what are the costs in case an immediate support of the vendor is required?

New business requirements

Another example in which the ITPfM methodology will show to be of great value is the situation that new requirements are added by the business process/function an IT portfolio supports. This can be triggered by business opportunities in the market (changes in customer demand), or legal obligations by governments (e.g. SOx controls, Basil II etc.) or clever sales/marketing of vendors.

In any of the cases above it's important to understand what the key driver is for making a changes to the IT landscape; one way or another there must be an added value as discussed in Chapter 3. In return it is very important to be able to inform them what the financial impact is of the new requirements. With these 2 insights clearly stated in a Business Case, you are able to make a sensitive decision on what to do. In any case it's very important to be able to outline how much the current IT landscape (portfolio or system) actually costs in the current situation. This must be in line with their expectations and *value* of the IT landscape. It is therefore always good to meet with the business users regularly to discuss the value of a portfolio or systems for them. This is not always easy to do (as discussed in chapter 3; how do you for example determine the value of an HR system?), but for good ITPfM practice it helps to make these type of discussions more concrete. For example; if the business value of an IT systems is set on EUR 100.000,- it doesn't make sense to just replace it with a new technology that costs EUR 500.000. As basic as this may sound, in many organizations this, the business value of an IT system, is not clear.

In addition to the above, ITPfM will also be helpful when evaluating different IT solutions that will meet the new business requirements. It is at the end all a matter of making a business requirement concrete (in money terms if possible) which will enable you to verify them against solutions offered by different vendors.

Cross portfolio technology integration

With the ITPfM methodology in place and all trusted sources contain all the key information about all components within all your IT portfolio's within your IT landscape, you are now also able to make cross portfolio reviews and comparisons on technology, function and components.

This can be in different areas. What you can for example to is to compare the sales systems between 2 (or more) different business processes/portfolios. There might for example be possibilities to merge, consolidate and integrate them into a single sales system, or perhaps just aligning on vendors (in case they are different) could save complexity and costs are perhaps there are now 2 separate support teams for both systems which have similar skills that can be merged into a central team.

Another area can be the ability to make architectural decisions on larger applications based on actual cost data. Especially in the ERP area, which typically is complex in structure and costs the ITPfM methodology can help to capture all relevant costs and make comparison between ERP's possible. With a central data structure in your CCS adequately applied, you will be able to compare large complex systems among themselves, but also to compare them with relative smaller systems.

A third area is the alignment of licenses between the different portfolios. For example the Microsoft Office license is in many organizations still separately determined and paid. Once you have insight in all your IT software components, you will also for example have clarity on which version or release they are running Microsoft Office (2003, VISTA, 2007 or 2013). For each of these versions you have to pay a license to Microsoft. It might therefore be better to select a single version for your organization and ensure all computers are running only on that version. This will make IT simpler to control and therefore cheaper to run.

Cross portfolio cost reductions

Another example what can be done with the ITPfM methodology in place is to do a cross portfolio review on all IT components, like servers, databases, firewalls etc. You will, for example, be able to create a single list in which all the servers in your landscape together with all their attributes (datacenter, OS release, etc). It will be a good practice to ask each Portfolio Team to do some famous “Zombie Server Hunting” (a Zombie Server being a server that runs in your IT landscape, is paid for each month, but nobody in the organization knows what it is doing there). Almost guaranteed you will find a number of servers that can be classified as zombie server and therefore can be reduced or decommissioned. Knowing that a server costs on average (depending on a lot of factors) between EUR 5.000 and EUR 10.000 per month; reducing 10 zombie-servers will save you between EUR 50.000 to EUR 100.000 per month on just that.

Like this there are many areas where costs can be reduced when viewed in a collective manner.

Chapter 8 Key benefits of ITPfM

Once all IT portfolios are aligned with the business processes and functions and all central systems are in place, the ITPfM methodology starts working and the first benefits of it will become visible. Obviously you'll have a total integral cost picture of all IT costs in your whole organization in place without redundancy or multiple versions of the truth. It also will bring the following key benefits that your organization will absolutely profit from.

Insight in IT costs

The first benefit ITPfM brings is insight into the actual IT costs in each ITPfM Quadrant Block of the portfolio. This should be monitored on a periodic basis; monthly is a good frequency as it is short enough to spot early signals things go wrong and long enough to also being able to focus on efficiencies. On a quarterly basis the Portfolio team can review the total costs in CCS for the whole portfolio. On a yearly basis all portfolios can be reviewed by the central ITPfM team and the top management of the organization. With the actual cost insight in place not only do you know what you spend the IT budget on, it will also give other benefits.

Ability to trade of new opportunities (projects)

A second important benefit of having ITPfM in place is the ability to adequately access if new products of vendors will actually help you to reduce your IYT costs or if it will increase your IT costs. As stated in the beginning of the book, in many cases new products are purchased with the idea to reduce costs for the organization, but in many cases turn up to actually increase the IT costs. With the ITPfM methodology in place not only do you know how much IT components or applications costs; you also have more insight in the costs elements; so any trade off for a new product can be better done on factual data. Specially the costs related to Run and Maintain the new components or applications are always difficult to pin down when discussing new offers, but with a solid ITPfM central systems in place, this can now history and you'll be in a lot better position to negotiate costs down.

Efficiency in projects and operations and cost reductions

The third major benefit of having the ITPfM methodology in place is that you have insight in all IT components that you have running in your landscape and therefore now can verify what is actually needed to run your organization. In a lot of different areas within IT efficiencies can be made.

For example you can compare portfolio's that use similar technology and components and determine if support or other activities can be combined. Maybe it is even possible to start running 2 or 3 processes on the same IT landscape instead of keep running in on 2 or 3 similar landscapes.

Another example is software licenses. In many cases you'll come to understand that because of the different IT departments working with the same partner; your organization end up paying double or triple for the same license. It can also be the case that you find out you run parts of your IT software with out of date licenses and compensation claims from vendors can be expected.

Ability to keep your landscape as "evergreen" as you want to afford

This is maybe the most important benefit that the ITPfM methodology brings you at the end; you will be able to make a clear and factual assessment of the state of your IT landscape and the need to update it to later versions; without being the

helpless victim of your vendors who off course emphasize the importance of being up-to-date with the latest releases. You can start creating roadmaps of your applications and systems in which is captured on which version of the underlying components and technology they are running.

Summary of part 3

In this section of the book you've read about how the ITPfM methodology could be rolled out in your organization. It also described the importance of trusted sources in which all high quality IT data must be captured (CAS, CIS, CPS, CTS). This may take quite some effort to accomplish and a lot of emphasis must be laid upon getting this in place as all next steps depend on this data. Furthermore you have read about the applications and benefits that the ITPfM methodology brings you. Start today by doing the Quick Self-Assessment in chapter 2.

Conclusion

With an ever faster growing development in IT systems it is very important for companies and organizations to keep up with these developments to at least keep up with the competition. What, however, is equally important is to keep understanding the "why" behind investments decisions. Too many times IT systems are purchased upgraded without a clear vision and sense of added value.

This book is written with the aim to make (IT) managers aware of how control can be gained back and how to evaluate what value IT systems bring to your organization. The Integral ITPFM methodology is designed to help (IT) managers to go through this journey. It is not a quick and easy journey, but once made, you will be a lot better equipped for the economic future with all its ups and downs. Good luck!!!

Quick Self-assessment

Now you have almost finished this book it might be interesting to test if you, with the knowledge that you have gained by reading this book, would give different results to the self-assessment you have done in chapter 2. Perhaps, while reading this book, you already did start to think differently about your IT landscape and perhaps already did start looking for the answers to the questions. That is great! The aim of writing this book is to help you start getting grip on your IT costs and the first step is to actively look for how much the components in your landscape actually cost. You can use the self-assessment form on the next page and again verify the results in appendix 1. When comparing the results of the two self assessments you will spot differences which will provide you with the insight in what you picked up on while reading this book and perhaps are the key areas that you need to focus on.

Nr	Question	Answer
1	How many employees are employed within your organization?	o < 50 o 50-250 o 250 – 500 o > 500
2	How many employees are employed within IT within your organization	o < 50 o 50-250 o 250 – 500 o > 500
3	How would you rate the size of your total IT landscape	o Almost no IT o Small o Medium o Large
4	What is the percentage of total IT cost vs total costs within your organization?	o <10% o 10% – 30% o 30% - 60% o 60%
5	Are all IT budgets managed centrally within your organization?	o Yes o No
6	Are there many major IT projects taking place in your organization?	o Yes o No
7	Are there many changes in the market your organization participates in?	o Yes o No
8	Are you able to determine how many servers your IT landscape contains within 3 days?	o Yes o No
9	Does your Enterprise IT landscape contain multiple ERP systems (of different vendors)?	o Yes o No
10	Does your Enterprise IT landscape contain different versions of Microsoft (or related software packages) for day-to-day business?	o Yes o No

Table 2 – ITPfM Quick Self-Assessment ©

Now that you have read the book and (hopefully) started to get insight in your IT costs and value, you might have the need for more specific information on any of the subjects described in this book. More information can be found on the website: www.itpfm.com. But there is also a blog & Facebook page in which different topics are discussed in more detail and with real life examples to help you making the right steps. This blog can be found at **www.adeniet.blog.com**

Let us know how you are doing with ITPfM!

We are also very interested in your own experience with managing IT costs with the ITPfM methodology. Please share them with us on the blogs, our online questionnaire on www.itpfm.com or send us an email ***contact@itpfm.com***

Part 4 Appendix

ITPfM Self-Assessment Results

Nr	Question	Answer	Score	Your score A	Your score B
1	How many employees are employed within your organization?	o < 50 o 50-250 o 250 – 500 o >500	1 point 3 points 5 points 10 points	☐	
2	How many employees are employed within IT within your organization	o < 50 o 50-250 o 250 – 500 o > 500 (10	1 point 3 points 5 points 10 points	☐	
3	How would you rate the size of your total IT landscape	o Almost no IT o Small o Medium o Large	1 point 3 points 5 points 10 points	☐	
4	What is the percentage of total IT cost vs total costs within your organization?	o <10% o 10% – 30% o 30% - 60% o 60%	1 point 3 points 5 points 10 Points	☐	
5	Are all IT budgets managed centrally within your organization?	o Yes o No	10 points 0 points	☐	
6	Are there many major IT projects taking place in your organization?	o Yes o No	10 points 0 points		☐
7	Are there many changes in the market your organization participates in?	o Yes o No	10 points 0 points		☐
8	Are you able to determine how many servers your IT landscape contains within 3 days?	o Yes o No	0 points 10 points		☐
9	Does your Enterprise IT landscape contain multiple ERP systems (of different vendors)?	o Yes o No	10 points 0 points		☐
10	Does your Enterprise IT landscape contain different versions of Microsoft (or related software packages) for day-to-day business?	o Yes o No	0 points 10 points		☐
Total Scores				☐	☐

Guide - how to use the ITPfM Self-Assessment questionnaire and process results

This chapter will guide you step by step through the ITPfM Quick Self-Assessment questionnaire and the next steps for projecting your results in the *ITPfM Cost Control Quadrant.*

Step 1: Fill in the questionnaire in Chapter 2 of this book by crossing the best suitable answer to the related question for your organization. In case you don't have an overview of the total organization, you can also apply it to your own IT department/team. *You can only use/cross one answer per question.*

Please note that you should answer the questions without verifying the answers/results later in this book as the whole point of this assessment is to capture the current "as-is" situation within your organization, not the desired one.

What is also important is to remember is that there is no "Right" and "Wrong" in any of your answers. This is just a high level assessment of the current situation of control on IT costs and expenses within your organization. There is no science behind it. The sole purpose of the assessment is to give an indication and awareness of how much control your organization has on IT costs.

Step 2: Once you have crossed all 10 answers of the assessment, you can go to the appendix Self-Assessment results (page 64 of this book) to determine what the scores of your answers are. You can do that by filling in the number of points assigned to the answer you entered in the boxes on in the right column (A or B).

Step 3: Add up all points in the right columns which gives you a total score between 0 and 50 per variable A or B.

Step 4: Use these scores to determine the position the *ITPfM Cost Control Quadrant below.* Your score (in the form of a point or dot) will be in one of the 4 quadrants of the ITPfM Cost Control Quadrant.

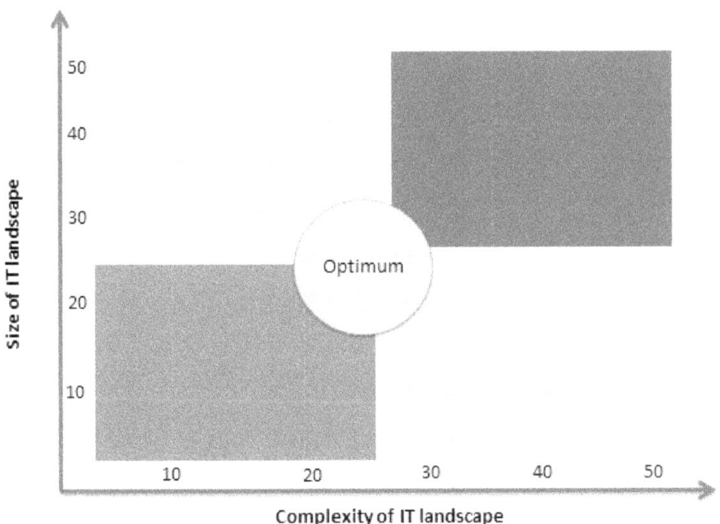

Step 5: Interpretation of the score in the ITPfM quadrant

Green Quadrant: If you score is in the bottom left (green) quadrant: this indicates that your organization is quite in control of IT Costs and Expenses. This doesn't mean its all perfect, but the "boat is at least not sinking." There is always room for applying ITPfM methodology for your organization, but the expected benefits are not major.

Yellow Quadrant: If your score is on the top left or bottom right (yellow) quadrants, your organization has lost at least some control on its IT costs and expenses and using the ITPfM methodology is already advised. A deeper analysis must be done on the actual situation and potentially some interesting results can be expected from using the ITPfM methodology.

Red Quadrant: If your score is on the top right (red) quadrant, there are strong indications that IT costs and expenses are not in control. ITPfM can be applied to start getting control on them. Organizations in this situation will gain the most of applying the ITPfM methodology.

Index of Topics

BCc: Business Capability Current (Page 30); variable of the ITPFM IT Value Model

BCo: Business Capability Optimized (Page 31); variable of the ITPFM IT Value Model

Business Process and Function (Page 27)

Cost Control Quadrant (Page 20)

CAS: Central Application System (Page 59)

CCS: Central Cost System (page 63)

CIS: Central Investment System (Page 61)

CPS: Central Project System (Page 60)

CTS: Central Technology System (page 58)

E: Business Process Efficiency (Page 30); variable of the ITPFM IT Value Model

I: Business Capability Increase (Page 30); variable of the ITPFM IT Value Model

Integrated ITPFM Value/Cost Model (Page 26)

ITPFM Methodology (Page 23)

IT-IPM: IT Investment Portfolio Management (Page 35)

IT-TPM: IT Technology Portfolio Management (Page 39)

IT-PPM: IT Project Portfolio Management (Page 40)

IT-STM: IT System Portfolio Management (Page 37)

IT-TCM: IT Total Cost Management (Page 41)

ITPFM Quadrant (Page 33)

ITPFM Quadrant Block (Page 35)

ITPFM IT Value Model (Page 31)

L: Legal Requirements (Page 30); variable of the ITPFM IT Value Model

Value/Cost trade-off (Page 28)

About the Author

Arthur de Niet is an Industrial Engineer who has worked 15+ years in the Oil and Gas industry in different IT management functions across the world.

One of his key drivers is to make people more cost aware in both business and in private live as in our modern society businesses and people can't live just "on the wind" anymore so they need know the basics about money and how to keep in control over it. Despite all the financial books written about this subject, many people and business are still struggling or making the wrong decisions based on wrong information.

This book was written with the intention to share his knowledge and experiences about managing IT costs in larger organizations by using IT units/portfolios that support specific business processes; which proved to be very successful.

If you are interested in getting in contact please send an email to: adeniet@itpfm.com

Notes

www.ingramcontent.com/pod-product-compliance
Ingram Content Group UK Ltd.
Pitfield, Milton Keynes, MK11 3LW, UK
UKHW021654190726
13853UKWH00001B/244

9 789082 483918